Learn with Me: Ready to Write

Carson-Dellosa Publishing LLC
Greensboro, North Carolina

Credits

Content Editor: Joanie Oliphant

Copy Editor: Sandra Ogle

Layout Design: Lori Jackson

Spectrum
An imprint of Carson-Dellosa Publishing LLC
PO Box 35665
Greensboro, NC 27425 USA
www.carsondellosa.com

ISBN 978-1-936024-76-6

335107811

Table of Contents

Dear Family Member,

Welcome to *Learn with Me: Ready to Write*. You and your child are about to start on a new adventure. Research tells us that knowledge of prewriting concepts, the willingness to try writing and drawing, and the strength and control to use crayons, markers, scissors, and other writing tools are important skills for children who are getting ready to enter kindergarten. Young children should develop the understanding of positional concepts, such as top, bottom, left, right, and middle. They should be able to produce accurate strokes, such as horizontal, vertical, and diagonal lines, curves, circles, and so on, as these are the basis of numbers and letters.

Learn with Me: Ready to Write has been written for families whose children have not yet been to kindergarten. This book contains tasks that involve coloring, cutting on lines with scissors, tracing with a finger, a pencil, or a crayon, and gluing. Each activity is designed to foster the development of skills, such as eye-hand coordination and small muscle (fine motor) development; grasping crayons, pencils, and scissors; and following verbal directions. While the activities promote multiple aspects of development, they are also designed to be fun and engaging for young children.

This is a "togetherness" book. Every activity is meant for families and children to work on together. Preschoolers need your guidance, support, and participation. After all, you are your child's first teacher. As you work, watch for the following significant areas of development: Your child will be developing "handedness," which is the use of a more dominant hand while still using both hands effectively. Your child will begin to understand and use positional words such as *above*, *below*, *left*, and *right*. Activities such as Setting the Table and Things Used by Firefighters are designed to promote this skill. You can reinforce these concepts with simple songs and games. Many activities, such as Blueberry Pie and Timid Turtle, are designed to increase your child's ability to produce basic writing strokes. Your child's attention and memory skills will develop as a result. Use the alphabet cards at the end of the book to introduce your child to tracing letters. Then, use them to play memory games to build awareness of initial sounds in words.

As you learn together, focus on having fun and on the excitement your child feels upon mastering new skills. You will be spending your time in the valuable pursuit of developing prewriting skills that will result in increased kindergarten readiness.

Enjoy learning together!

The Spectrum Team

Directions: Cut out the insect pictures. Follow the steps to glue the pictures near or on the mushroom.

Step 1: Glue the worm in the middle of the mushroom.

Step 2: Glue the ant next to the mushroom.

Step 3: Glue the grasshopper next to the mushroom.

Step 4: Glue the dragonfly above the mushroom.

cut

Setting the Table

Directions: Cut out the pictures. Place a small paper plate on a table.
Follow the steps to set the table.

Step 1: Place the fork on the left of the plate.

Step 2: Place the knife on the right of the plate.

Step 3: Place the spoon on the right of the knife.

Step 4: Place the cup above the plate.

Step 5: Place the napkin below the plate.

Things Used by Firefighters

Directions: Cut out the pictures. Follow the steps to make the picture on another sheet of paper.

Step 1: Glue the fire truck in the middle of the paper.

Step 2: Glue the hat above the fire truck.

Step 3: Glue the boots below the fire truck.

Step 4: Glue the coat on the right of the fire truck.

Step 5: Glue the fire hose on the left of the fire truck.

cut

Who Is My Mother?

Directions: Cut out the pictures. Match the baby animals with their mothers. Trace the lines between the matching pictures with your finger and with a pencil.

cut ✂

Directions: Cut out the pictures. Match the pictures at the top with the pictures at the bottom. Glue the matching pictures together on another sheet of paper. Trace the lines between the matching pictures with your finger and with a pencil.

cut

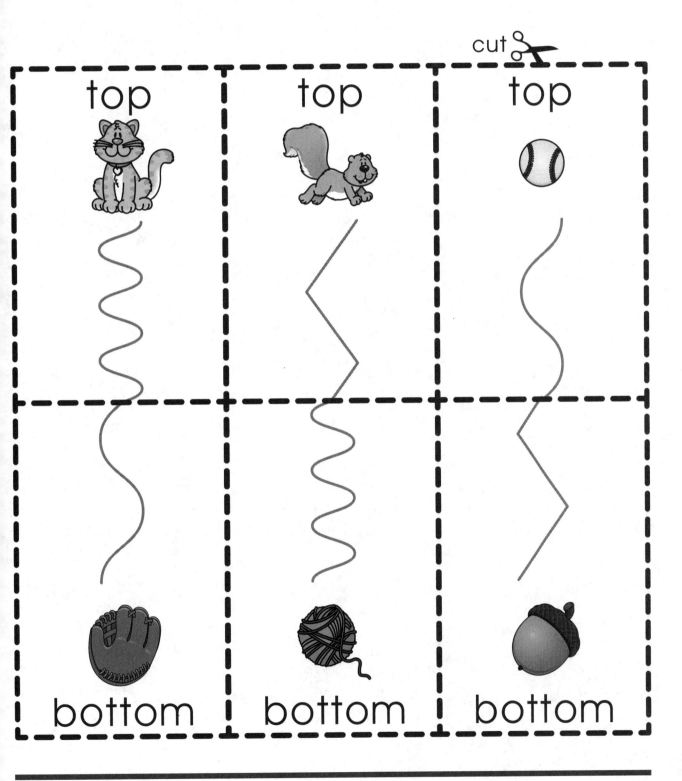

top

top

top

bottom

bottom

bottom

Directions: Trace the road sign shapes. Cut out the road signs. Tape each sign to a wooden craft stick. Insert your signs into small balls of clay to make them stand. Use the signs when playing with small cars and trucks.

The Barnyard

Directions for the Barn: Cut out the barn. To make it stand, fold a 1 ½" (3.8 cm) wide piece of card stock in half. Match the bottom edge of the barn to the fold of the card stock. Glue the barn to the card stock above the fold.

Directions for the Animals: Cut out the animal cards. Fold the cards along the fold lines so that the animals can stand. Practice placing the animals to the left, right, top, and bottom of the barn. Tell an adult where you place each animal.

cut

cut

fold   fold   fold   fold

Directions: Trace the lines on the picture frame with your finger and with a pencil. Color the frame. Decorate it. Cut out the frame's outside edge along the dotted lines. After an adult cuts out the center, place a photograph facedown on the back of the frame. Tape it in place.

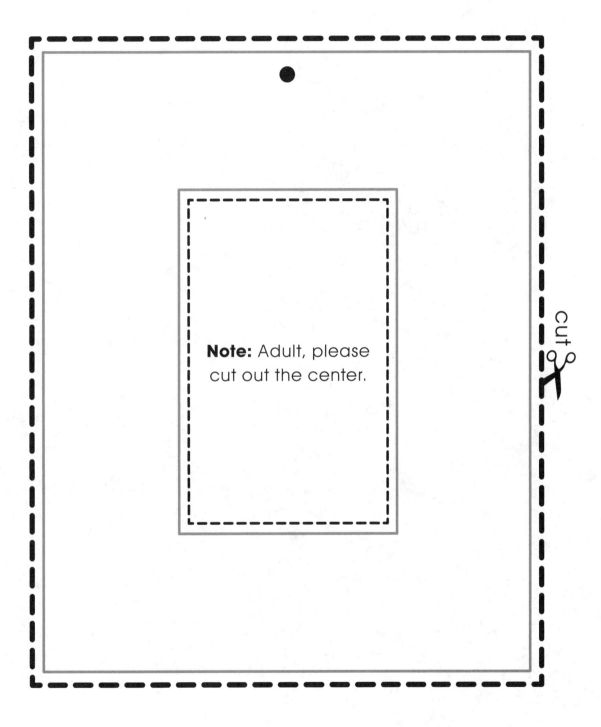

Note: Adult, please cut out the center.

cut

Day and Night Wristbands

Directions: Color the suns and the moons. Cut out each wristband. Ask an adult to help you wrap one around each wrist. Overlap the ends. Tape them together.

cut

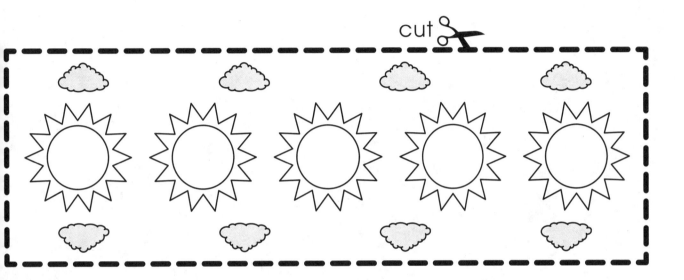

cut

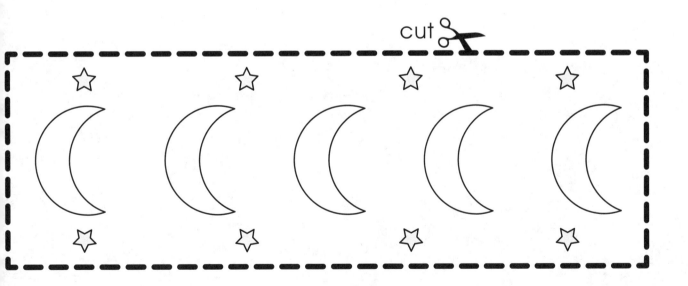

Directions: Trace the stripes on the clown fish with an orange crayon. Cut out the clown fish and the box around the sea anemone. Cut the slits on the anemone. Hide the clown fish in the anemone by weaving it between the slits.

cut

cut

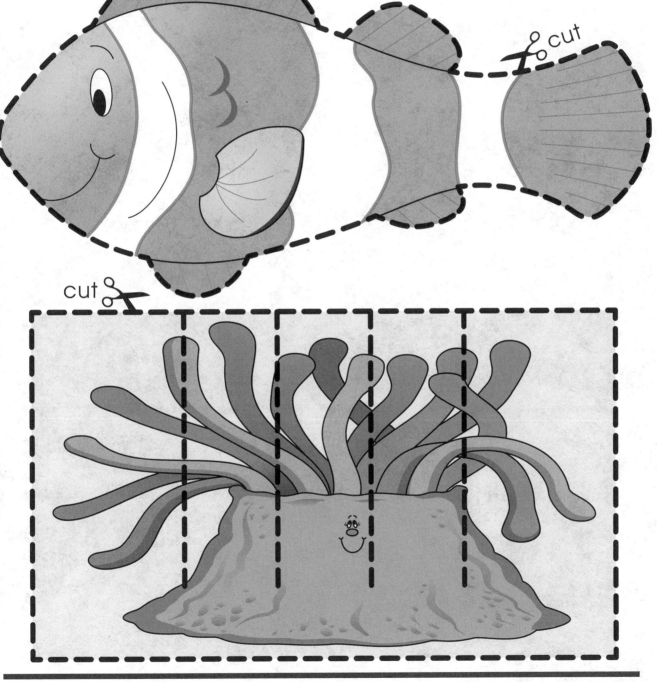

Shapes Puzzle

Directions: Color the shapes. Cut out the puzzle pieces. Arrange the pieces. Glue the completed puzzle to another sheet of paper.

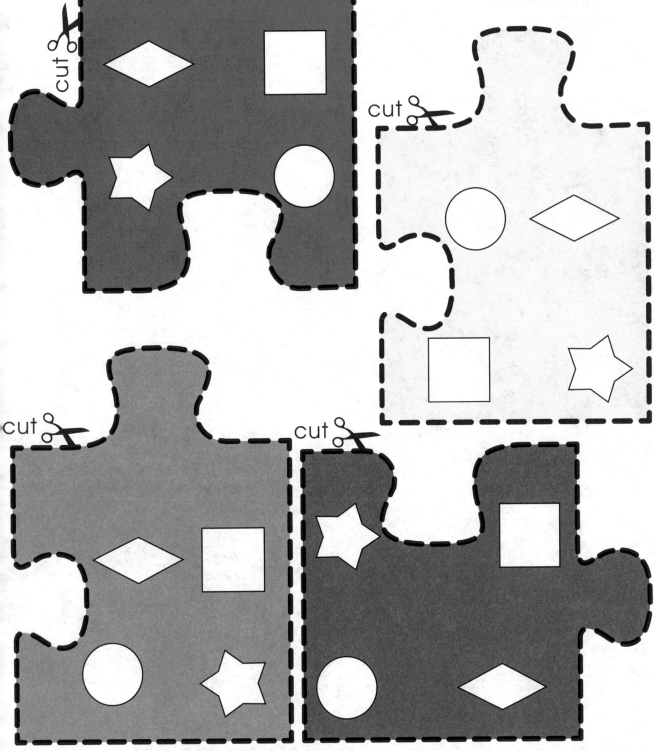

cut

cut

cut

cut

25

Three Houses

Directions: Cut out the houses. Glue them to a sheet of card stock. To make the houses stand, fold the page border under. Fold the houses on the fold lines.

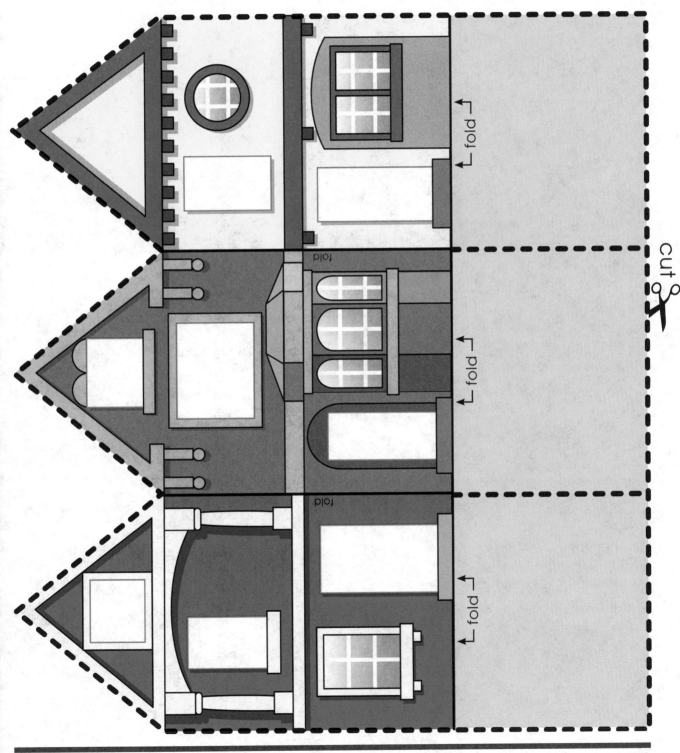

Lightning in the Cloud

Directions: Trace the bolts of lightning. Color them with a yellow crayon. Cut out the lightning bolts. Fold a sheet of paper in half. Place the cloud pattern on the fold. Trace and cut out the cloud. Color it with a gray crayon. Glue a small piece of aluminum foil over the cloud's center. Glue the lightning bolts to the cloud.

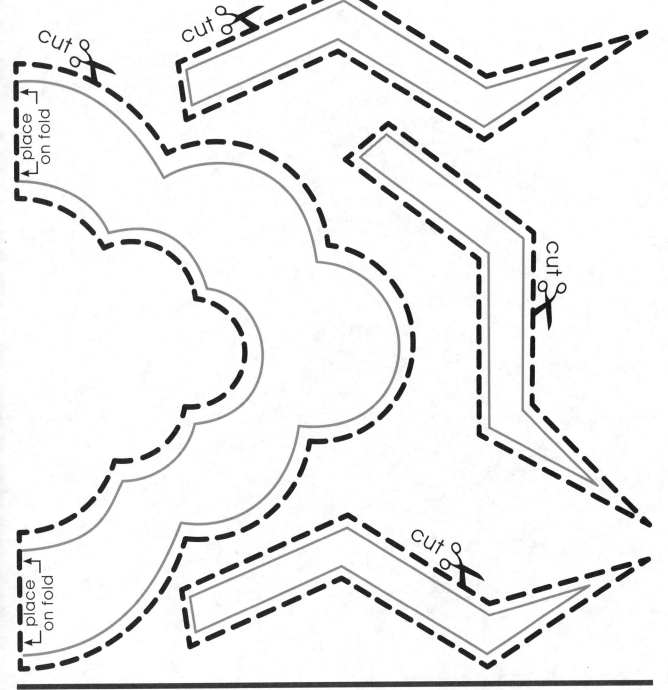

cut

cut

place on fold

cut

place on fold

cut

Polly the Parrot

Directions: Trace the triangles on the crackers. Trace the numbers inside the crackers. Cut out the crackers and the parrot pattern pieces. Use the picture to help you glue the parrot pattern pieces onto a plastic cup. Place the crackers in the cup. Pull out a cracker. Pretend to feed it to the parrot as you read its number.

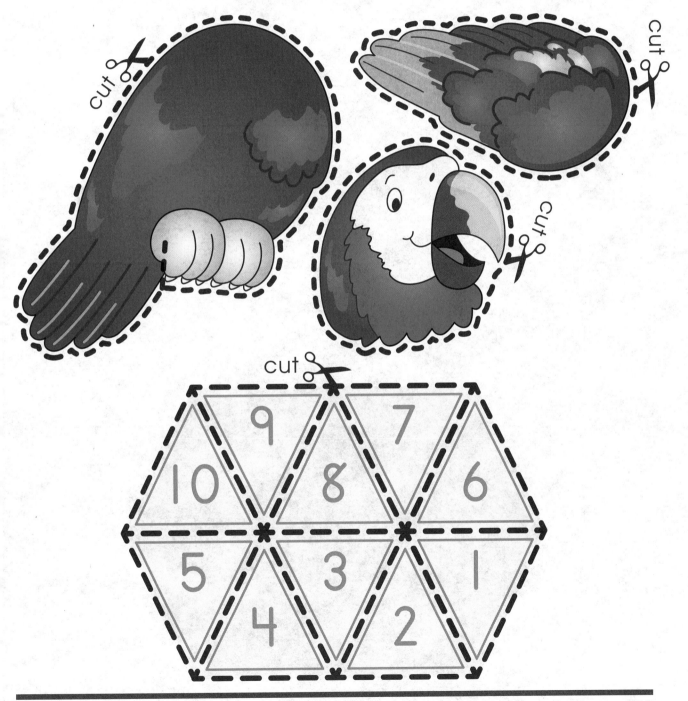

Sailboats

Directions: Trace the sails on each sailboat with your finger and with a pencil. Color the sailboats. Cut a lake shape from a large sheet of blue construction paper. Cut out the sailboats. Glue the sailboats on the lake.

cut ✂

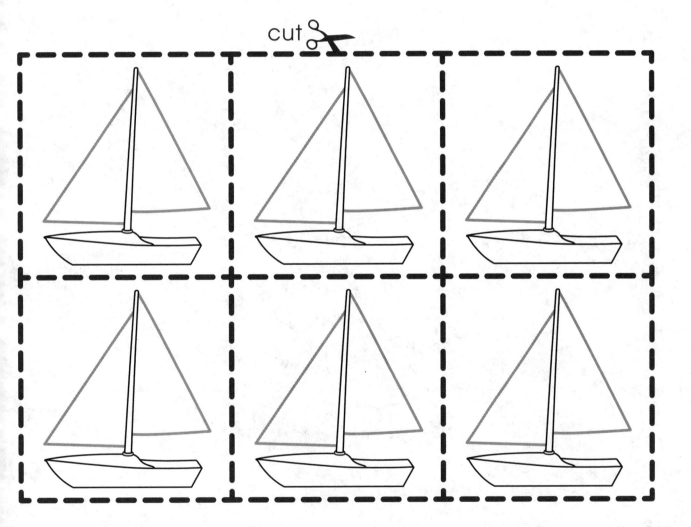

Spiderwebs

Directions: Trace the path from each spider to its web with your finger and with a pencil. Cut out the pattern. Trace the pattern eight times on a large sheet of paper. Cut out the pieces. Arrange them in the shape of a spiderweb. Glue the spiderweb onto black or brown construction paper. Decorate your spiderweb by tracing the lines with crayons or markers.

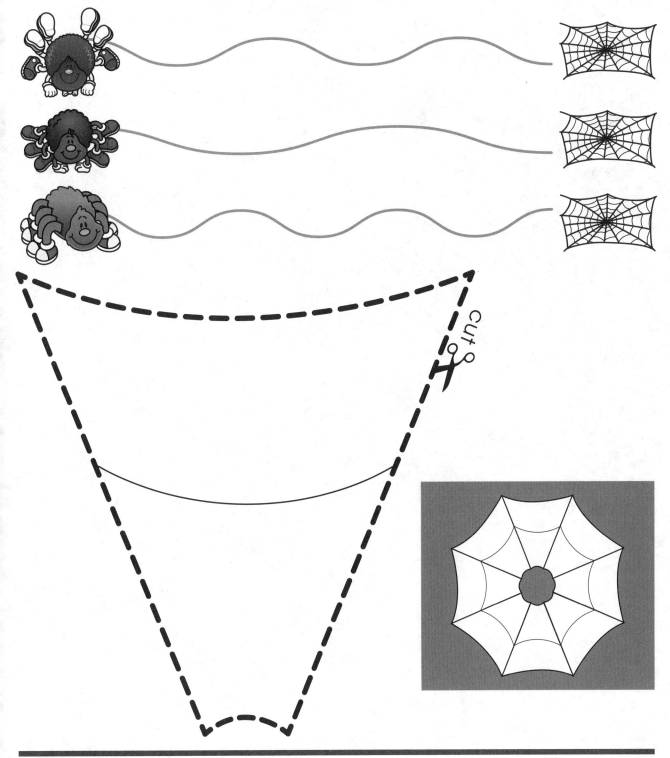

Cut

Directions: Trace each blueberry with your finger and with a pencil. Color them blue. Cut out the blueberries and the slice of pie. Glue the blueberries on the pie. Glue the pie to a paper plate or a circle of white construction paper.

cut

cut   cut   cut   cut

cut   cut

Hatching Chicks

Directions: Trace the zigzag line on each hatching egg with your finger and with a pencil. Cut out the eggs. Cut out the chick pattern with the help of an adult. On another sheet of yellow construction paper, trace the chick pattern eight times. Draw a triangle beak and eyes on each chick. Glue one egg on top of each chick. Display your picture of hatching chicks.

cut

cut

cut

cut

cut

cut

cut

cut

cut

A Slice of Watermelon

Directions: Trace the watermelon shapes below with your finger and with a pencil. Draw some watermelon shapes. Trace the watermelon seed shapes with your finger and with a pencil. Cut out the watermelon seeds. Cut a paper plate or a circle of white construction paper in half. Color it red and green to look like a slice of watermelon. Glue the seeds on the watermelon.

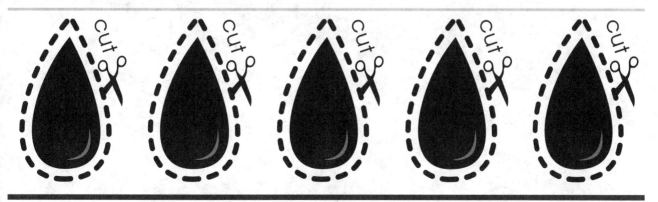

Directions: Trace the upside-down U shapes on the turtle's shell. Cut out the turtle. Tape the turtle on a wooden craft stick to make a puppet. Fold under the turtle's head, legs, and tail to make him go into his shell to hide.

cut

Fish Friends

Directions: Trace the fish with your finger and with a pencil. Color the fish. Cut out each fish. Glue the fish to a large sheet of blue construction paper to make an aquarium. Add foil bubbles, plants, and a diver or treasure chest to the aquarium.

Directions: Trace the circle and the lines on the flower with your finger and with a pencil. Color the flower. Cut it out. Glue the flower on a large paper plate or a circle of white construction paper. Glue sunflower seeds in the flower's center. If desired, add a stem made from a strip of green construction paper.

cut

Note to Family Member: The ball box is used with the activities on pages 51 and 53. It is intended that an adult make the box prior to working on the driving activities. The box holds a small ball.

Directions: Trace the grid pattern on a sheet of construction paper or card stock. Use the notches to help you as you draw the grid lines. Fold on all horizontal and vertical lines. Cut four lines as far as the central square as shown. Glue the flaps with the lowercase letters in back of the flaps with the uppercase letters. To use the box, place it over the ball and roll the box along a track.

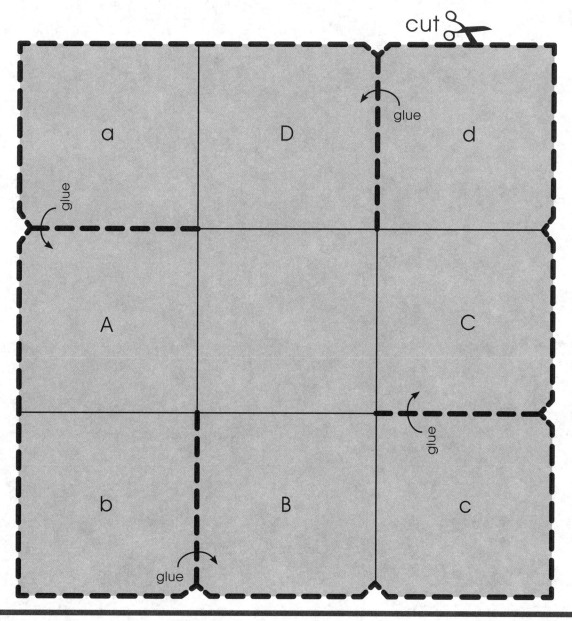

Note to Family Member: In advance, make the ball box using the pattern on page 49.

Directions: Trace and cut out the road with adult help. Fold a sheet of construction paper in half each way. Place the cut-out road pattern on the folds. Use a white crayon to trace the lines in the middle of the road. Cut out the cars. Glue or tape them to opposite sides of your ball box. Place the box over a small ball. Use the car to practice driving along the road.

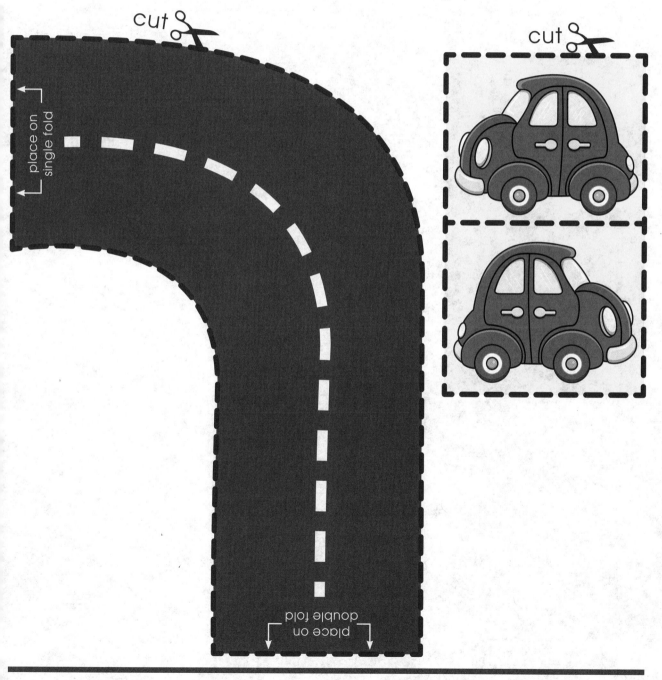

cut

place on single fold

cut

place on double fold

Driving the Train

Note to Family Member: In advance, make the ball box using the pattern on page 49.

Directions: Trace and cut out the track with adult help. Fold a sheet of construction paper in half each way. Place the cut-out railroad track pattern on the folds. Cut out the trains. Glue or tape them to opposite sides of your ball box. Place the box over a small ball. Use the train to practice driving along the railroad tracks.

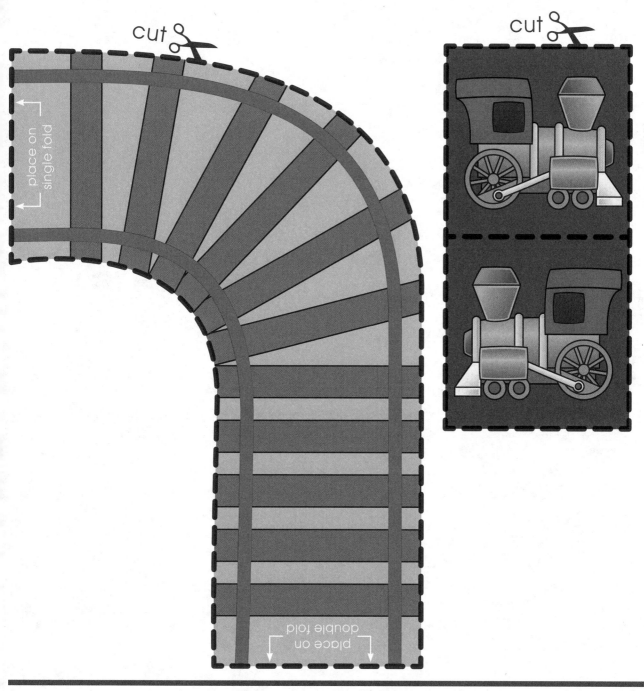

Directions: Trace the letters with your finger and with a pencil. Cut out the cards. Use them with the other cards to learn how to read and write the letters.

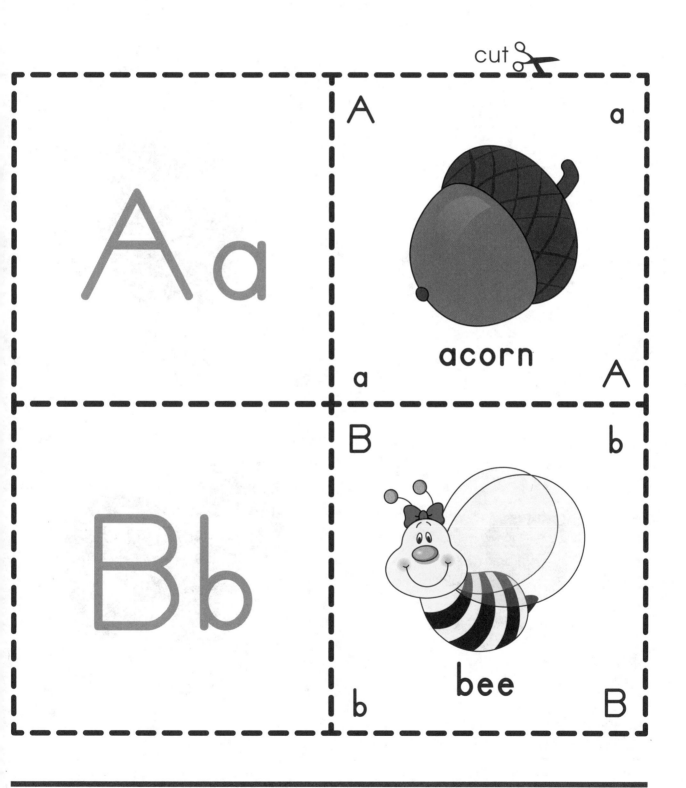

cut

A   a

acorn

a   A

B   b

bee

b   B

Aa

Bb

cut

A   a

apple

a   A

Aa

B   b

bear

b   B

Bb

Directions: Trace the letters with your finger and with a pencil. Cut out the cards. Use them with the other cards to learn how to read and write the letters.

cut

C c

C c

car

C c

D d

D d

duck

d D

cut ✂

C ∣ c

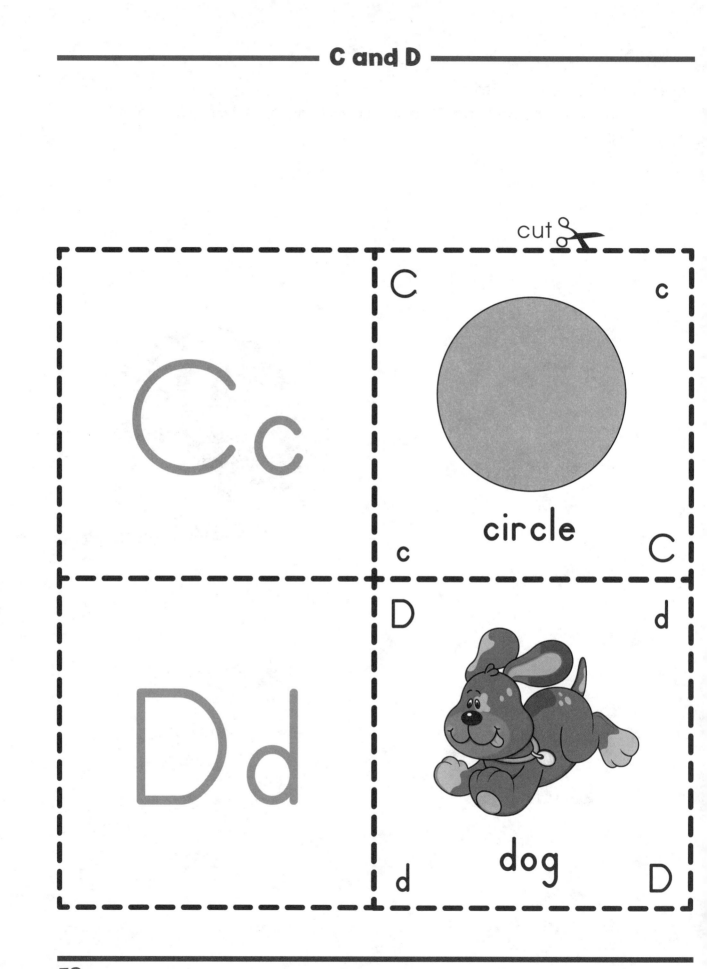

circle

c ∣ C

Cc

Dd

D ∣ d

dog

d ∣ D

Directions: Trace the letters with your finger and with a pencil. Cut out the cards. Use them with the other cards to learn how to read and write the letters.

cut

E   e

E e

elephant

e   E

F f

F   f

feather

f   F

cut

E   e

eagle

e   E

E e

F   f

F f

fish

f   F

Directions: Trace the letters with your finger and with a pencil. Cut out the cards. Use them with the other cards to learn how to read and write the letters.

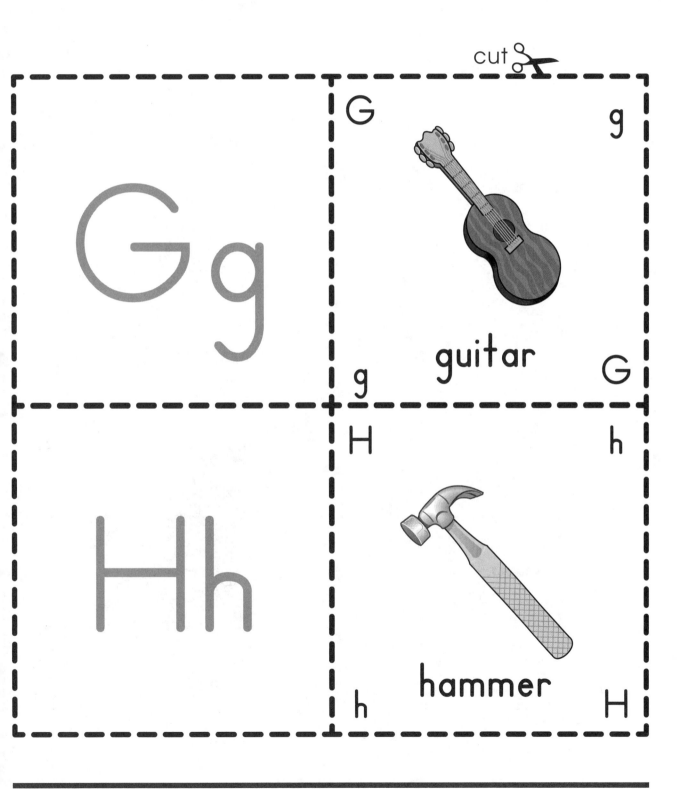

cut

G   g

Gg

guitar

g   G

g   H   h

Hh

h   hammer   H

cut

G g

G

g

giraffe

g

G

H

h

Hh

horse

h

H

Directions: Trace the letters with your finger and with a pencil. Cut out the cards. Use them with the other cards to learn how to read and write the letters.

cut ✂

I   i

igloo

i   I

J   j

jar

j   J

I i

J j

cut

I   i

ice cream

i   I

Ii

J   j

Jj

juice

j   J

Directions: Trace the letters with your finger and with a pencil. Cut out the cards. Use them with the other cards to learn how to read and write the letters.

cut

K   k

K k

k   K

kangaroo

L   l

L l

L   L

lion

l

cut

K   k

key

k   K

Kk

L   l

Ll

ladybug

l   L

Directions: Trace the letters with your finger and with a pencil. Cut out the cards. Use them with the other cards to learn how to read and write the letters.

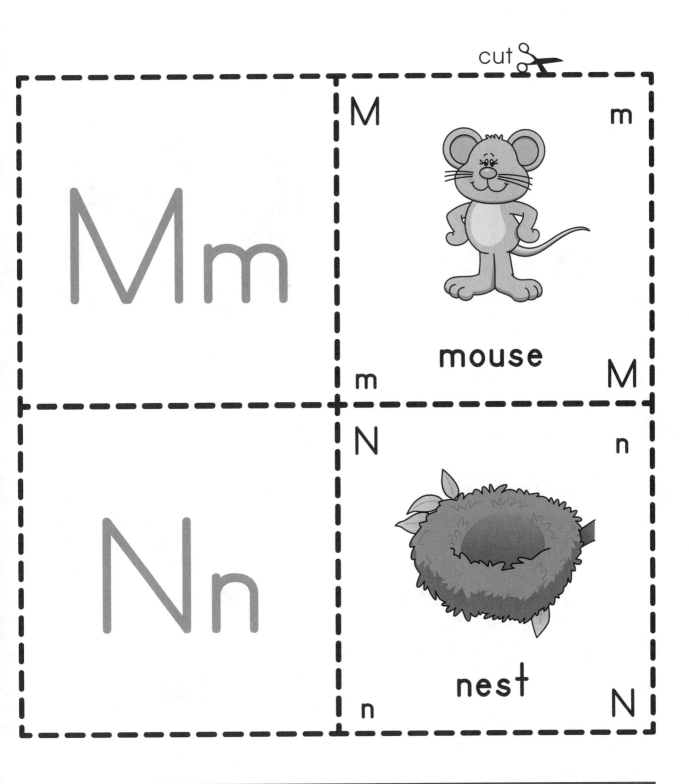

cut

M   m

mouse

m   M

N   n

nest

n   N

cut

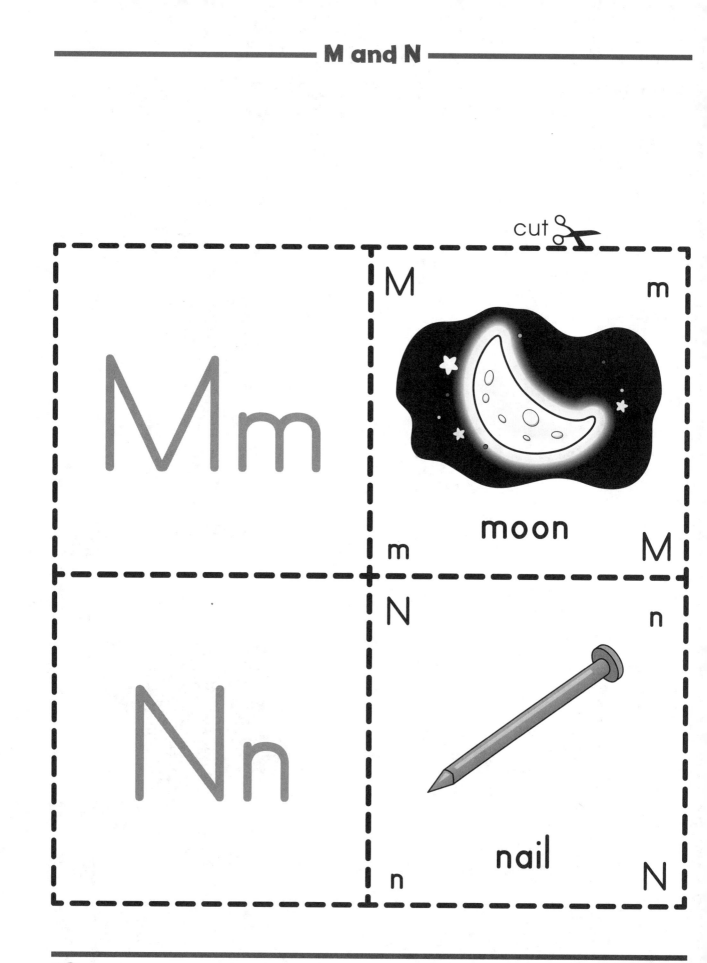

M   m

moon

m   M

N   n

nail

n   N

Directions: Trace the letters with your finger and with a pencil. Cut out the cards. Use them with the other cards to learn how to read and write the letters.

cut

O   o

ostrich

o

O

P   p

P   p

p

pear   P

cut

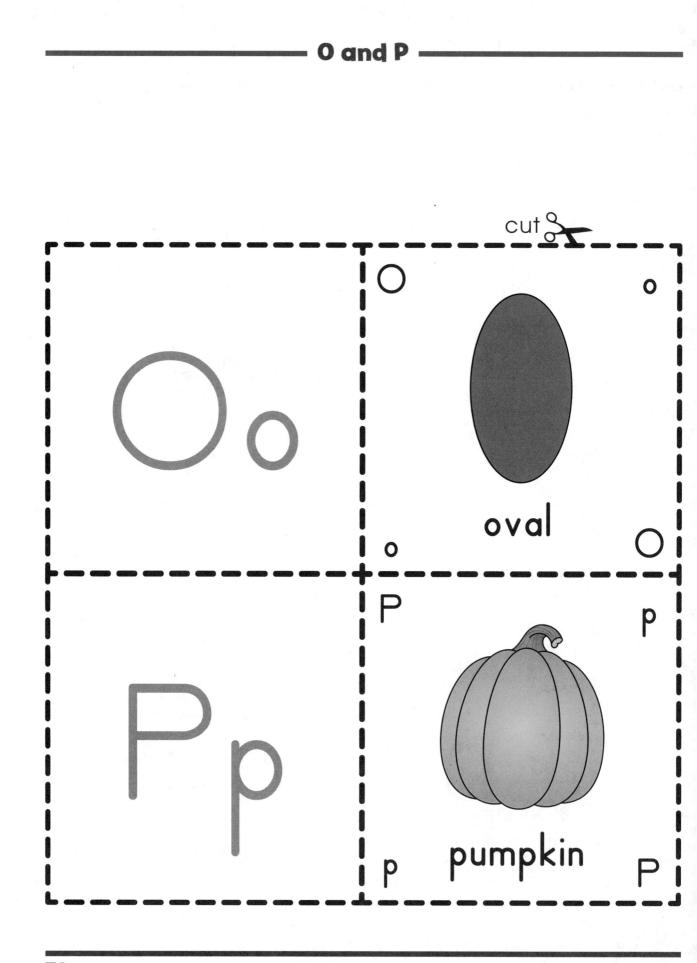

O   o

oval

o   O

P   p

p   P

P   p

pumpkin

Directions: Trace the letters with your finger and with a pencil. Cut out the cards. Use them with the other cards to learn how to read and write the letters.

cut

Q   q

quilt

q   Q

R   r

rabbit

r   R

cut

Q   q

queen

q   Q

R   r

R   r

rainbow

r   R

Directions: Trace the letters with your finger and with a pencil. Cut out the cards. Use them with the other cards to learn how to read and write the letters.

cut ✂

S s

s

S

S s

sock

T t

s

T t

t

T t

tiger

t

T

cut ✂

S   s

sun

s   S

T   t

turtle

t   T

Ss

Tt

Directions: Trace the letters with your finger and with a pencil. Cut out the cards. Use them with the other cards to learn how to read and write the letters.

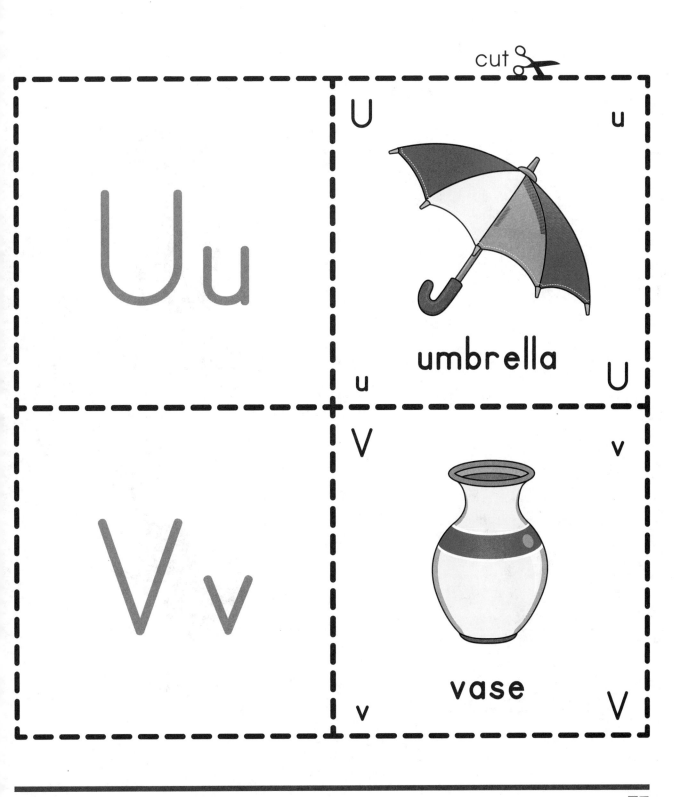

cut

U u

U u
umbrella

u U

V v
vase

v V

V v

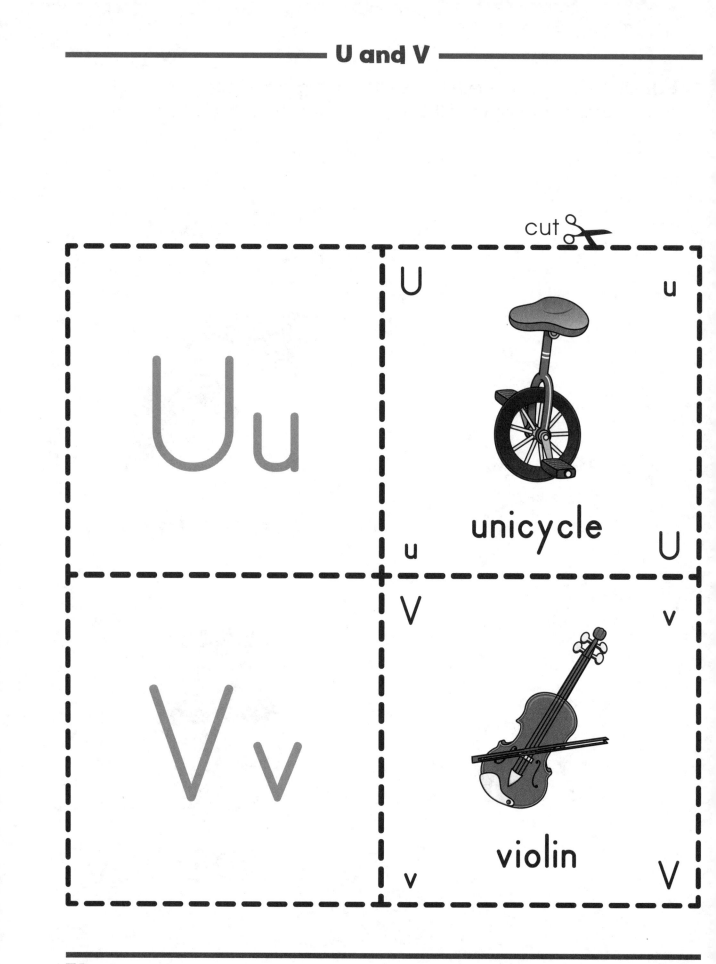

cut

U   u

unicycle

u   U

V   v

violin

v   V

Directions: Trace the letters with your finger and with a pencil. Cut out the cards. Use them with the other cards to learn how to read and write the letters.

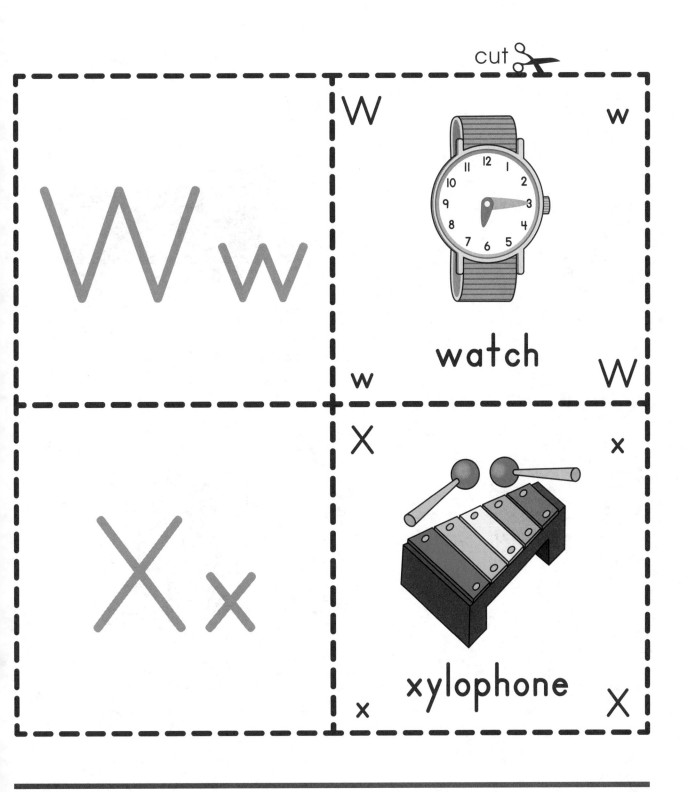

cut

W   w

W w

w   W

watch

X   x

X x

xylophone

x   X

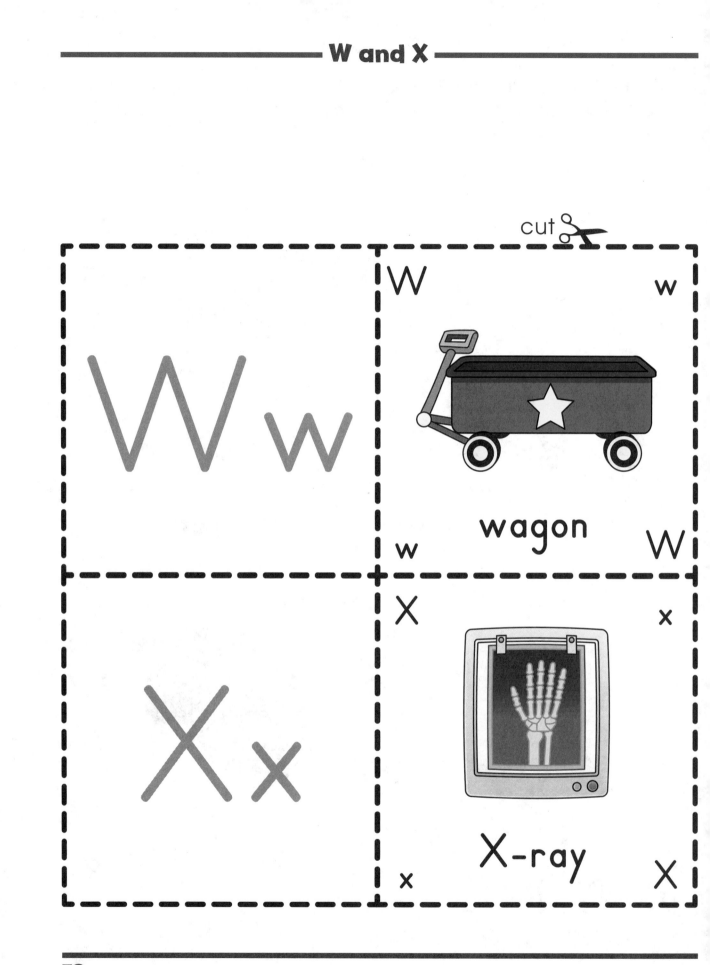

cut

W   w

W   w

wagon

w   W

X   x

X   x

X-ray

x   X

Directions: Trace the letters with your finger and with a pencil. Cut out the cards. Use them with the other cards to learn how to read and write the letters.

cut

Y   y

yo-yo

y   Y

Z   z

zebra

z   Z

cut

Y   y

yak   Y

y

Z   z

zipper

z   Z